Contents

G000060017

Inside Front Cover: St.Aubin on the Hill, The Glass Rainbow
Front Cover: St.Martin's Church, The Sacrifice of Isaac (detail)

St.Ouen's Manor Chapel, St.Anne (detail)

Preface

This guide book is an introduction to the life and work of a remarkable but little-known Jerseyman, the stained glass artist Henry Thomas Bosdet (1856–1934).

It is published in the hope that his talent will receive greater recognition among a wider public, both in the Island and abroad. As you discover the beauties of his windows, you will see that he deserves no less.

Some thirty of Bosdet's windows, only a part of his total output, can be seen in our Island churches. Another six are to be found in the private chapel of St Ouen's Manor and the house itself has a number of Bosdet's windows portraying the history and armorial bearings of the de Carteret family. All are described and catalogued for the first time in this new guide. All have now been photographed in detail by the author and many are reproduced to illustrate this work.

*For my lovely Judy to whose patience, confidence and
discernment this book, and I, owe so much.*

A few words of advice

When you set out, do take a small pair of pocket binoculars with you. They make all the difference, especially when you are discovering the finer details of Bosdet's windows.

If possible, choose bright weather (not necessarily sunny) to appreciate the full brilliance of Bosdet's glass.

Allow yourself time and calm to explore the windows and, if you like, read the appropriate passage from a pew Bible, for which references are given in part three of this guide. The texts and the windows will complement each other and enrich the experience for you.

Don't forget to enjoy the churches, too! They are treasures in their own right of which the glass is but a part. Many of them are early medieval foundations which embody much of our Island's history and have been the fountain of its spiritual life over many centuries. Their intimate proportions and the relative darkness of their interiors make them ideal settings for the jewel-like quality and intensity of colour of Bosdet's glass. They contain fascinating details of all sorts, including many noteworthy stained glass windows by other nineteenth and twentieth century designers whose story, however, falls outside the scope of this present guide.

Find the East

To make it easier to follow the indications given in part three of this guide, remember that Christian churches are normally built with the chancel and high altar pointing to the east. In most cases, the font is installed at the west end.

Access

You will find most of Jersey's churches open for prayer and visiting between the hours of nine and late afternoon. There is, of course, no charge for entry but you may want to show your appreciation by making a voluntary offering towards maintenance and restoration. Please do not circulate in a church if a service is in progress.

Stained Glass

Glass, that extraordinarily versatile and beautiful material which we take so much for granted, has a history going back at least six thousand years. In the fourth millennium BC, the Egyptians were already using it for small dishes and phials. By the time of Christ, the technique of glass blowing had been developed in Syria and wealthy Romans were beginning to glaze their window apertures with slab glass.

Glass in Britain was first mentioned by the Venerable Bede and excavations in the North of England have corroborated his testimony by recovering fragments of coloured glass from the sites of seventh century Saxon monastic houses.

Because of its translucent qualities, glass was attributed a mystical character which made it entirely appropriate for the embellishment of churches. The secrets of its metamorphosis from a fusion of sand, potash and oxides to gem-like glass were jealously guarded and made it a costly commodity. Its use expanded nevertheless and later architectural developments such as flying buttresses, which permitted large, glazed apertures in church walls, helped produce the medieval glories which adorn our great Gothic cathedrals. The processes involved in the manufacture of stained glass have changed little over the centuries. Of necessity, this is but a brief and very much simplified description of a complex and fascinating craft, but further reading is suggested in the bibliography. The clear, viscous substance is produced by heating sand and potash to a high temperature. It is coloured by the addition of various metallic oxides: copper for green, cobalt for blue, selenium for red, manganese for purple and so on.

The liquid coloured glass is blown into long balloon shapes which are then cut down the length, flattened out horizontally and left to cool. Further colour effects can be obtained by 'flashing', the dipping of clear glass into molten glass of another colour. When fired, this produces glass of layered colours. Parts of the upper layer can be removed by acids, revealing the colour beneath.

The artist, who is usually helped by a team of craftsmen at various stages of the process, produces initial working sketches (called "vidimus") for the design and eventually a full-size detailed drawing (cartoon) of the intended window. Coloured glass is cut into appropriate shapes to fit the many areas of the design and these are laid out on the flat surface of the cartoon. Until the late Middle Ages, glass cutting was most laborious, being carried out with a tool called a grozing iron. The introduction of the diamond cutter in the sixteenth century speeded this process along greatly. All parts of the glass jigsaw are then joined together and soldered into thin strips of lead called calms (pronounced 'cams'). In spite of its vulnerable appearance and its flexibility, the completed window is astonishingly robust and large areas of glass can be assembled in this way.

Details in the design, such as facial features, shading and decorative patterns on fabrics, are painted or stippled onto the glass before the joining-up stage. The artist uses a medium made from iron oxide and ground glass which he applies like paint, using various types of brushes or sponges. This is then fired in a kiln and the painted detail is fused permanently with its glass base.

The stained glass window is supported in the wall aperture by horizontal metal rods, called saddle bars, set in the stonework on either side at approximately twelve inch intervals. To protect stained glass from damage, either from the elements or from accidental or wilful harm, many churches nowadays cover the outside of the glass with secondary glazing or at least with a wire mesh. In general, stained glass windows need a complete overhaul every hundred years or so. This is a laborious and costly process which, however, must be programmed and budgeted for if our wonderful heritage of stained glass is not to deteriorate and disintegrate. It is a heavy financial burden for today's congregations to bear and both public and private sponsors are to be encouraged to invest in this worthy cause. The ecclesiastical authorities, supported and advised by competent experts in the field, will be vigilant, as their forefathers were in the past, to ensure that new glass installed in our ancient churches or restoration work on existing glass will be of the finest design and highest quality.

Opposite: St.Brelade's Church, The Sower (detail)

The Bosdet Family

It is a strange fact that you will not find the name BOSDET listed in the current Jersey telephone directory. In the eighteenth and nineteenth centuries, however, it was to be found in the rates lists and census returns of many Island parishes, with perhaps more numerous mentions in St Peter, St Lawrence and, of course, St Helier.

Today, Bosdets are to be found in many parts of the world, from Australia to Florida, from Mexico to the Gaspé Peninsula of North America. The Bosdets who are interested in genealogy look to Jersey as the cradle of the family. Although the name is first recorded in the late Middle Ages, it is with Jacques Bosdet, born in Jersey in 1779, that most contemporary Bosdets claim a link.

This patriarch, Jacques, married three times. His second wife, Jeanne Coignard, whom he married in St Clement's Church, Jersey, in 1808, bore him seven children, of whom the sixth, Thomas, born in 1822, the future master mariner, was destined to be the father of Henry Thomas, artist and subject of our present study, born in 1856.

After the death of his first wife, Sophia Le Roy, in 1859, Captain Thomas Bosdet married her sister Emmeline in 1861, who thus became Henry Thomas' stepmother. This couple had a son, Edgar, Henry Thomas' half-brother.

Sadly, Henry Thomas' line of the family was not to endure. In marked contrast with his grandfather, Henry Thomas had only one child, Harry Westropp Bosdet, born in 1916, who was to lose his young life in action during the Normandy landings of June 1944.

Henry Thomas Bosdet Curricum Vitae

1856   7 January. Born in Hampton Place, The Parade, St Helier, Jersey. Parents: Thomas, master mariner, of Jersey and Sophia Mary, née Le Roy, of Guernsey. The birth certificate states that the childwas delivered by his mother and that she registered his birth. From a Lloyds Register of Captains, we know that the father was born in Jersey on 11th September 1822, his father being Jacques, according to the Parish Rates list, and his mother being Jeanne Coignard, second wife of Jacques.

1859   31 July. Sophia, Henry Thomas' mother, died at sea of typhus fever, on her husband's barque "Ellen", and was buried in Jersey 20 September, at St Saviour's Cemetery.

1861   18 March. Henry Thomas' father, Captain Bosdet, married Emmeline, Sophia's sister, in St Clement Danes, Westminster. Emmeline thus became stepmother to the five year old Henry Thomas Bosdet.

1869/71   Pupil at University College School, now at Hampstead but then at Gower Street, London.

1873   10 January. Henry Thomas enrolled as a student at the Royal Academy, at the age of 17. (Source: Royal Academy)

1882   Living at 54 Patschull Road, Camden. He supplied a window of the Crucifixion to Ste. Marie du Câtel Church, Guernsey. (Ref.Jersey Heritage Archive). At this time, he was teaching at the Islington College of Art, also known as the Barnsbury School of Art, in Barnsbury Hall, and was mentioned in a press report of a prize giving in 1882 and in a school programme of 1884.

1883   Appointed Curator of Life School at the Royal Academy. (Source: Royal Academy)

1885   He exhibited an unnamed portrait at the Royal Academy.

Henry Thomas Bosdet with his father Captain Thomas Bosdet and his stepmother Emmeline Le Roy. Probably 1861

1898 22 June, he married Julia Marion Reece Edwards, a widow, in the Marylebone Registry Office, (Info: Free BMD). The marriage certificate gives his residence at the time of marriage as 20 Newman Street, Marylebone. One of the witnesses was Adelina Bosdet Webber, the other being her husband. The couple moved to Inglewood, Grove Park Terrace, Chiswick during this year and remained there until 1910. This address is inscribed on a number of his stained glass windows. In this same year, he addressed the Jersey Society in London, of which he was a member, on "Art Ancient and Modern" (Bulletin of Jersey Soc.London).

1901 The 1901 Census described Henry Thomas Bosdet as stained glass artist, 45 years of age, working at home on his own account, married to Julia Marion, aged 48. From other sources we know that she was née Reece Edwards, daughter of a deceased barrister, born in Devon. The Jersey Heritage Trust possesses a letter dated 15 July 1901 from Ernst Crofts of Burlington House, praising Henry Thomas' long service as Curator of the Life School of the Royal Academy.

1902 He joined the Société Jersiaise and was a member for the remainder of his life.

1903 The "Sporting Life" of 23 May comments upon Bosdet's recent window at Kingsclere Church. near Newbury, (Soc. Jers. Bosdet scrapbook).

1904 31 August. Death of Bosdet's father, Captain Thomas Bosdet, of cancer, in Grouville, in his eighty-second year. Buried in St Saviour's Cemetery, Jersey (Registrar, Royal Square, Jersey).

1905 Bosdet completed the Great West Window of Hexham Abbey.

1906 He completed the Dean Farrar Memorial Window, Hexham Abbey.

1907 Bosdet painted the reredos for St Saviour's Church, Jersey, depicting the Nativity of Christ.

1908 Bosdet completed the Fairless Memorial Window, Hexham Abbey.

1909 2 February. Death of Henry Thomas' wife, Julia Marion, aged 57. Buried in St Saviour's Cemetery, Jersey.

1911   Now at Bishopswood Studio, Brigwood Road, Hampstead Garden Suburb, Hendon, London NW4, where he remained until 1920 (Bull. Soc. Jers. List of Members). In these years, on a date we have not yet been able to establish, Henry Thomas Bosdet married his second wife, Mary Catherine Brereton, daughter of Dr William Westropp Brereton, Professor of Surgery at Queen's College, Galway.

1916   22nd May. Birth of Harry Westropp, Bosdet's only son, later killed in action, Normandy, 1944.

Left: Henry Thomas Bosdet as a young man

1917   Charles Henderson Memorial Window, Hexham Abbey. The window bears the inscription: H. T. Bosdet 1917, Brigwood Rd, London.

1918   10 April. Death of Henry Thomas' stepmother, Emmeline, aged 92, in Grouville, Jersey. Buried in St Saviour's Cemetery, Jersey.

1920   Bosdet resigned from Chairmanship of Council of Jersey Society in London and returned to Jersey. On 8 May, he bought Belle Vue Cottage, St Lawrence, and lived there until June 1927.

1925	3rd April. Bosdet made a will leaving his property to his (second) wife, Mary Catherine (née Brereton) and then to his son Harry Westropp Bosdet (Ref: Jersey Archive).
1927	25th June. Bosdet sold Belle Vue Cottage, St Lawrence (cf. deed of sale, Judicial Greffe, Jersey), and moved to France.
1928	The family was now living at 7 Cours d'Orbitelle, Aix-en-Provence (Bull. Soc. Jers.).
1929	Bosdet moved to 12 Cours Sextius, Aix-en-Provence. He was also there in 1930 (Bull. Soc. Jers.).
1931	The family left France and returned to Jersey, probably during the summer. Bosdet's son Harry was enrolled at Victoria College on 17th September and remained for two years.
1932	The family was living with a relative, J. H. Bosdet, at Beechwood, St Peter (Victoria College register).

St.Brelade's Church, The Good Sheperd (detail)

1933	Henry Thomas Bosdet rented Le Patrimoine, St Lawrence (Rates List, St Lawrence, Coin Motier Vingtaine).
1934	23 May. Bosdet died at Le Patrimoine, St Lawrence, aged 78 years. His funeral took place in St Saviour's Church on 25th May and he was buried in St Saviour's Cemetery (Evening Post). (St Saviour burial register 1934, page 210, entry 2108). His death certificate states that he died of 'bronchite, maladie du coeur' (bronchitis, heart disease), and is signed by Dr H. J. Blampied.
18 June	The minutes of the Comité Executif of the Société Jersiaise record as follows: "Le Comité a accepté avec remerciements l'offre généreuse de la part de Madame Bosdet, de donner à la Société une collection de dessins des vitraux peints, oeuvre de son feu mari, Monsieur H. T. Bosdet" (Bulletin Soc Jers. 1935). (The Committee has gratefully accepted the generous offer of Mrs. Bosdet to donate to the Société a collection of drawings of stained glass windows, the work of her late husband, Mr H. T. Bosdet.)

St.John's Church,
St.John The Baptist
(detail)

Henry Thomas Bosdet 1856 – 1934

The works of Henry Thomas Bosdet are one of the lesser-known treasures of Jersey, yet they are easily accessible every day in many of our Island churches and are looked at by thousands of residents and tourists every year. They are part of the wider collection of Bosdet's works which are to be found in numerous churches in England and abroad.

As public as his works are, Bosdet himself remains elusive and retiring. Details of his professional and private lives and insights into his creative thinking have proved difficult to find and gather. In spite of his obvious artistic and commercial success, he gives the impression of being a modest man who revealed himself with reluctance. We do know from various newspaper reports over the years that he was highly thought of as a man and artist.

At the time of writing, possibly the last living person to have known Bosdet is Miss Roza Alfreda Amy, born in 1910, whose father, Alfred Amy LRAM, an accomplished pianist of the late nineteenth century, was a good friend of Bosdet. She remembers seeing them meeting and talking together and describes Bosdet as tall, distinguished, sporting a goatee beard and 'dressed as an artist would'. This image is confirmed by a photograph of Bosdet, taken during a group visit of the Société Jersiaise to Trinity Manor, in 1906. He looks out at us with a gentle expression, his grey hair parted in the middle, appearing somewhat older than his fifty years at the time.

Henry Thomas Bosdet was born in Jersey on 7th January 1856, in a house forming part of Hampton Place, behind All Saints Church in the Parade. His parents were Thomas Bosdet, Master Mariner of St Helier and Sophia Mary, née Le Roy, of Guernsey, married in St Saviour's Church in 1854. She was the daughter of John Le Roy of Guernsey, an optician, now settled with his family at 15 Mulcaster Street, St Helier. Henry Thomas' birth certificate states that the mother delivered the child herself and that she registered the birth a week later.

We have little information about the very early years of Henry Thomas but we do know that they were marked by tragedy. His mother, Sophia, died at sea of typhus fever in July 1859, in the barque "Ellen" which was under her husband's command. We do not know if their son, Henry Thomas, two years seven months old at the time, was also a passenger on his father's vessel. Sophia's body was brought back to Jersey in the "Ellen" in September 1859 and buried in St Saviour's Cemetery. Two years later, his father, Captain

Bosdet, married Sophia's sister Emmeline Jones Le Roy, on 18th March 1861 in the Church of St Clement Danes, Westminster. Henry Thomas' new stepmother eventually gave the boy a half-brother, Edgar. The sea captain died in Grouville in 1904, in his eighty-second year, and his widow Emmeline died in the same parish in 1918, aged 92. Both are buried in the family grave in St Saviour's Cemetery.

The St Helier Parish rates list tells us that young Henry Thomas' family was no longer in Hampton Place by 1862. It was possibly around this time that the family settled in England. At the age of thirteen, Henry Thomas was enrolled as a pupil at University College School, Gower Street, London, a private school which later moved to Hampstead. By seventeen, he was a student at the Royal Academy.

A few years later, in 1882, Bosdet was teaching at the Islington College of Art in Barnsbury Hall. It is around this time that we have the first indication of his interest in stained glass for his window of the Crucifixion in Sainte Marie du Câtel Church, Guernsey, dates from the same year. In 1883, when Bosdet was 27, his talent in drawing was officially recognised for he was appointed Curator of the Life School at the Royal Academy, a post he held for the next sixteen years. He was the second of only two men to have held this title which, in 1903, was changed to Curator of the School of Modelling from Life. Although we have no details, we know that he showed his paintings at the Royal Academy Summer Exhibitions.

Jersey is fortunate in possessing one example of Bosdet's painting, the reredos behind the high altar in St Saviour's Church. It represents the coming of the shepherds and the Magi to pay homage to the newborn child Jesus. It dates from 1907 and each of the three panels bears Bosdet's signature. It is painted in Pre-Raphaelite style against a gilt background. The figures have the delicacy of drawing, the subtleties of colour and the spirituality which we associate with Bosdet's work.

On 22nd June 1898, Bosdet married Julia Marion Reece Edwards, a widow, in the Marylebone Registry Office. She was the daughter of a deceased barrister and was born in Devon in 1853. The couple set up home at Inglewood, Grove Park Terrace, Chiswick, the address which appears, along with his signature, on a number of Bosdet's windows. The 1901 census tells us that it was from this address that Bosdet worked at home on his own account as a stained glass artist.

St.John's Church, detail of Resurrection window

Bosdet kept in close touch with fellow-Islanders in England through his membership of the Jersey Society in London, founded in 1896. The Society's records show that he was Honorary Treasurer for a number of years and eventually became Chairman of the Council. He regularly proposed or made reply to the after-dinner toasts and, in 1898, he addressed the members on "Art Ancient and Modern". In 1902, he became an overseas member of the Société Jersiaise and remained committed to it all his life. A photograph in the Société's archives, taken in 1906, shows him with a large party of Société members visiting Trinity Manor.

St.Martin's Church, Nativity Window, Head of St.Joseph (detail)

His gifts as a stained glass painter and maker were very much in demand and his windows invariably won much praise. Most of his numerous Jersey windows were commissioned in the first two decades of the twentieth century. The "Sporting Life" of 23rd May 1903 commented very favourably on his new window in Kingsclere Church, near Newbury. In 1905, he installed the first of four important windows in Hexham Abbey, Northumberland. All were highly praised and considered to be much in sympathy with the architecture and stonework of the ancient building. Some of Bosdet's most prestigious work was commissioned by his cousin, Mary Sarah Aubin, who lived for many years in the Netherlands with her husband, John Edward Willem Twiss. Through her good offices and patronage, Bosdet designed a total of nine windows for Holy Trinity Anglican Church in Utrecht.

In February 1909, Bosdet's wife, Julia Marion, died and was buried in Jersey at St Saviour's Cemetery.

His increasing production required more working space and in 1911 he moved to Bishopswood Studio, Brigwood Road, Hampstead Garden Suburb. In 1912, he received an important commission from the then Seigneur of St Ouen's Manor, to design and install a series of windows in the Manor chapel, illustrating legends of the life of St Anne. A number of heraldic designs and illustrations of events in the history of the de Carteret Family were also completed by Bosdet to decorate the entrance and great hall of the manor itself.

Bosdet eventually married again, this time Mary Catherine (1877 – 1947), daughter of Dr William Brereton of Queen's College, Galway. At the age of sixty, Bosdet's life changed dramatically for he became a father. A son, Harry Westropp Bosdet, was born to Mary Catherine on 22nd May 1916. The boy's infancy was spent in London but he came to live in Jersey with his parents on Bosdet's return to his native Island in 1920. Harry was educated at the Jersey Modern School (1925 – 1927), in the Lycée of Aix-en-Provence (1927 – 1931) and later at Victoria College, Jersey (1931 – 1933). From the Victoria College Book of Remembrance we learn that Harry's life ended tragically. He was killed in action at twenty-eight years of age and is buried in the Commonwealth Cemetery near Bayeux.

At the age of sixty-four, Bosdet retired from his active life in England. He resigned from the Chairmanship of the Jersey Society in London and returned to Jersey. In the same year, he bought Belle Vue Cottage, St Lawrence, and resided there with his family for the next seven years. In 1927, he sold this house and went to live in France at various addresses in Aix-en-Provence. We can surmise that this decision was prompted by ill health, but, in reality, we possess little detailed information of this period of his life.

In 1931, Bosdet brought his family back to Jersey and stayed with a relative, J. H. Bosdet, at Beechwood, St Peter. Later, he rented Le Patrimoine, St Lawrence, from Mr F. Edouard Bisson.

It was in Le Patrimoine that Bosdet died on 23rd May 1934, aged 78. His death certificate states that he died of "bronchite et maladie du coeur" (bronchitis and heart disease). On the next day, the "Evening Post" marked the sad event with a brief summary of his work which included the following eulogy: "The deceased, who was a native of Jersey, was famous for his

exquisite work, examples of which are to be seen in many of the cathedrals and churches on the mainland. It may indeed be said that he was at the very top of his profession, and for years was on the staff of the Royal Academy where hundreds of pupils passed through his hands."

The funeral service took place in St Saviour's Church and the interment was in the family grave on the northern perimeter of the churchyard. His widow and his son Harry were present, as well as a number of his local friends including representatives of the Société Jersiaise.

In the June following Bosdet's death, the minutes of the Société Jersiaise Executive Committee record the passing of a vote of thanks to his widow for the generous gift to the Société of a large collection of Bosdet's drawings and designs. The full-size cartoons, now in the care of the Jersey Heritage Trust, are of great beauty and, along with his windows in our churches, bear a moving witness to the exceptional talents of this distinguished son of Jersey.

Opposite: Gouray Church, Jesus in Gethsemane (detail)

Henry Thomas Bosdet's Works in Jersey

To our forbears of the seventeenth and eighteenth centuries, our Island churches today would appear colourful, frivolous and 'popish' places. They knew only buildings of austere, whitewashed plaster, with clear glass in the windows, dark box pews and high galleries, with little religious decoration in evidence.

Since the Reformation in the sixteenth century, Jersey had largely followed the Calvinist tendency which eradicated all remnants of Catholic practice in liturgy, symbolism, church furnishings and ornamentation.

This situation changed radically and rapidly from the middle of the nineteenth century. In 1833, John Keble founded the Oxford Movement which advocated the revival and restoration of the ancient liturgy and practices of the medieval church in England. From their publications, the supporters of change became known as Tractarians. Both nationally and locally, debate was fierce and sometimes acrimonious. The Jersey newspapers of the time reveal, for example, that the installation of the East window in St Luke's Church (map ref .6) in 1852 was the subject of powerful protests which, however, did not prevail. Important changes took place as more and more clergy and congregations, led at national level by Edward Pusey and John Henry Newman, espoused the reformist stance. The process was accelerated by the construction of numerous new churches in the rapidly developing industrial regions, many of them designed by the Catholic architect A. W. N. Pugin, and also by the new interest shown in the restoration of ancient and dilapidated churches, chapels and monasteries, as promoted, in particular, by The Society for the Protection of Ancient Buildings, founded by William Morris in 1877.

This movement brought about dramatic transformations in church decoration and ceremonial. Whitewashed plaster, box pews and galleries were removed, new church furnishings were installed, stained glass windows were commissioned to replace clear glass, and altar curtains, banners and liturgical vestments were re-introduced. The second half of the nineteenth century was a particularly flourishing time for designers and manufacturers of all things ecclesiastical. The newly introduced practice of installing stained glass windows as family memorials greatly accelerated the demand for this medium and many new firms were founded. Henry Thomas Bosdet's work was a continuation of this wave and contributed to it, not by any particular innovations, but by the importance he attached to tradition, both in artistic expression and in the techniques of glass manufacture and painting.

His style owed much to the Pre-Raphaelite Brotherhood, a group of artists who lived and worked in London from 1848 onwards. The Brotherhood, founded by John Everett Millais, William Holman Hunt and Dante Gabriel Rossetti, looked to medieval art for inspiration and painted principally literary and biblical scenes. Their influence on Bosdet can be seen in the medieval idiom of his windows and in his lyrical draughtsmanship.

Cartoon for Annunciation window in St.Martin's Church (detail)

As far as can be ascertained from his dated signatures on the windows, from the dates included in the memorial inscriptions or from the minutes of the Ecclesiastical Court, which granted faculties for the installations of stained glass windows, most of Bosdet's creations in Jersey were commissioned in the years between 1898 and 1930. His window in Guernsey's Câtel Church is much earlier, dating from 1882. Twenty-two of Bosdet's Jersey windows are signed, most in the lower right hand corner and, of these, fifteen are dated. Bosdet designed a total of thirty-three windows for Jersey churches, to which must be added the two windows exhibited in the Jersey Museum, six windows in St Ouen's Manor Chapel and an important collection of secular stained glass in the manor itself.

Bosdet's work is outstanding, not only for the rich nuances of colour in the glass but also for the quality of his drawing and the balance of his compositions. More perhaps than that of many of his contemporaries, his work has a rare spiritual quality which reveals the artist's deep reverence for the sacred stories and characters he depicted.

His sensitive portrayals of Christ, the Virgin Mary and the disciples never descend into sentimentality. The beauty of his figures is neither effeminate nor flamboyant. Gestures are restrained but filled with significance. Facial expression is controlled yet eloquent, benign yet powerful. Bosdet's head of Jesus in the Last Supper window in St Lawrence's Parish Church is an outstandingly moving portrayal of the anguish of Christ before His trial, suffering and death.

With a few exceptions, Bosdet's windows in Jersey churches are inspired by New Testament stories. Most of the principal events of Christ's life are here, from the Nativity to the Ascension. The Annunciation is the most frequently depicted story, appearing with variations of detail in five churches, St Helier, St Martin, Holy Trinity, St Saviour and St Brelade. Old Testament representations are to be found in two buildings only, firstly, in St Martin's Church, in the form of the Sacrifice of Abraham in the South wall, the heads of three prophets high up in the Nativity window, and Sarah, Abraham's wife, above the Annunciation window and, secondly, in St Ouen's Manor Chapel, where King David, Abraham and the prophet Zephaniah are represented.

In general, the scenes are shown on one plane only, with little detail in the background to distract from the main characters. In-filling is invariably in the form of ornate architectural supports and canopies, decorated with stylised foliage in the medieval fashion. Occasionally, fruit and flowers are depicted in profusion. Although the sea appears in a number of windows, Bosdet did not attempt to draw on the local environment for decorative motifs. Neither is there any search for historic realism in terms of costume or location. Most clothing is sumptuous and richly decorated in a late Gothic or early Renaissance idiom.

Bosdet's work has a clarity of design which makes each window easy to 'read'. The eye of the beholder is taken gently around the composition, with little to divert his attention from the essence of the picture. The overall effect is generally static, calm and restful, with only an occasional hint at underlying drama and tragedy. Some of the characters look out directly at the viewer, engaging him or her immediately in the story, appealing as much to the heart as to the head.

The colours, though strong and richly varied, are essentially harmonious and reassuring. Along with the sensitivity of drawing, they create the atmosphere of reverence and serenity which each scene produces. The subtleties of tone introduced into his glass by Bosdet are notes upon which the light plays, giving rise to infinite variations as the sun travels across the sky. Bosdet's windows are in a state of constant change, enriching the light in our churches and bringing life to the granite. Ultimately, however, the success of stained glass is determined neither by the eloquence of its line nor the effect of its colours upon the eye but by the degree to which it prompts a soaring of the human spirit. We come away from Bosdet's windows enlightened and uplifted.

*Previous page: St.Ouen's Manor Chapel
small window of the Prophet Zephaniah*

*This page: St.Martin's Church
Annunciation Window (detail)*

Secular and Domestic Stained Glass

Although stained glass is principally associated with churches, many examples are to be found in Britain in civic and academic buildings as well as in great houses. Such windows usually portray historical figures, ancestors, founders, benefactors and favourite sons and are often richly decorated with coats of arms and other heraldic devices.

St Ouen's Manor in Jersey possesses a number of such windows, designed by Henry Thomas Bosdet. They were commissioned by the Seigneur of St Ouen in the early years of the twentieth century and record the feats of two of his famous forebears. The de Carteret Family has been identified with St Ouen's Manor since Norman times and is particularly known for its loyalty to the Royalist cause during the Cromwellian era in the seventeenth century.

Understandably, the domestic stained glass in this private house is not normally accessible to the public but the photographs in this book and the following brief description will give enthusiasts some idea of its richness of design and colour.

a) The principal example is a large rectangular window in the passage opposite the panelled drawing-room. It is divided into six panels of which the three upper ones are designed around the coat of arms of the Malet de Carteret Family. The surrounds are lavishly filled with wreaths, garlands, decorative devices and the family motto, in Latin and French, on scrolls and banners: HONOR, VIRTUS, LOYAL DEVOIR (Honour, Virtue and Loyal Duty).

The three lower panels depict incidents in the history of the Island. The centre panel shows a moment in 1518 when the Bailiff of Jersey, Sir Helier de Carteret, vindicated the independence of Jersey law against the English Governor, Sir Hugh Vaughan. This is a particularly crowded and colourful composition with many armed men surrounding the protagonists, against a background of a throne decorated with the Royal Coat of Arms. Through the open door, there is a glimpse of Grouville Parish Church, reminding us that the Court was sitting in that Parish because the plague was raging in St Helier. The side panels illustrate incidents during the French occupation of the Island in the middle of the fifteenth century.

On the left, Sir Philip de Carteret escapes from a French ambuscade by leaping his horse over the Val de la Charrière in 1463. This is a romantic illustration of chivalrous bravery, centred on the leap of the powerful horse. The darkness of his black coat is made all the more striking by the scarlet harness.

In the right-hand panel, under a Norman arch, the French Governor of Mont Orgueil Castle surrenders its key to a youthful Sir Philip de Carteret and Sir Richard Harliston in 1463. Sir Philip, very striking in a red tabard bearing his family arms, is surrounded by soldiers in armour, beneath a forest of lances, halberds and banners.

The window is signed H. T. Bosdet but the accompanying date is partly obscured.

b) The Manor hall and the great stairs.

Here the glass is purely heraldic and decorative. There are four windows on the left on entry, each with an upper and a lower panel. The four upper panels are of clear glass with inserts of flowers and foliage. The lower panels, also with surrounds of clear glass, depict coats of arms bearing the following names: a) St Ouen, b) Granville, c) Spencer and d) De Caux. Below these, the space is filled with elegant garlands of fruit and flowers, particularly dog roses.

The bay window at the foot of the stairs has a similar arrangement of glass. The three upper panels are filled with decorative motifs in grisaille (grey monochrome) and garlands in coloured glass. The lower panels again depict coats of arms, of which the middle one bears no name but depicts a crow, emblem of the Corbet family. The other two are respectively Lemprière and Sarre.

The first landing on the stairs is lit by a tall, rectangular window of three vertical panels. The upper one depicts the date 1906 in entwined figures in the centre of a laurel wreath, surrounded by garlands of fruit and flowers. The middle panel contains the Malet de Carteret arms and motto LOYAL DEVOIR (Loyal Duty), above the name of the Seigneur, E. C. Malet de Carteret. The bottom panel repeats the charming garlands of fruit and flowers.

The windows on the upper landing of the stairs revert to the pattern of those on the ground floor. The four upper panels continue the theme of flowers and fruit, as do the lower ones but with the addition of large Roman capital letters in the centre of each, M and C for Malet de Carteret.

In spite of the dark panelling in the hall, the mixture of clear and coloured glass in the windows creates a luminous and airy atmosphere. The frequently repeated garlands of fruit and flowers introduce a light and festive note, a feminine touch to balance the masculine coats of arms.

St.Ouen's Manor, Sir Helier de Carteret Window (detail)

St. Luke's Church, The Good Shepherd (detail)

Bosdet's Cartoons

Soon after Bosdet's death in 1934, his widow donated his collection of drawings to the Société Jersiaise. This princely gift is the other half of Bosdet's important legacy to this Island.

The collection of drawings includes over one hundred and forty items, ranging from simple initial sketches to full-size cartoons for very large windows.

Most are executed in pencil and many have been colour-washed to indicate the palette which Bosdet wished to use in any particular window. Designs for floral or architectural borders abound as well as angels, armorial bearings, elegantly flowing scrolls and lettering for memorial inscriptions.

The beauty of line and the sensitivity of Bosdet's portrayal of the many biblical characters in the collection are breath-taking. Unfortunately, due to the passage of time, many of the drawings are fragile and the collection is not normally on view. Restoration of a number of cartoons has begun, thanks to the generous sponsorship of the BNP Paribas Bank, St Helier. With the kind agreement of the Jersey Heritage Trust, a small selection of the cartoons has been especially photographed for this guide. They demonstrate eloquently Bosdet's outstanding graphic talents.

St.John's Church
(detail)

Bosdet at Work

One of Bosdet's most important commissions, four large windows in Hexham Abbey, Northumberland, was completed over some thirteen years at the beginning of the twentieth century. Contemporary accounts of this work, published in the Hexham Parish Magazine and in the Hexham Abbey Record, afford us some small insight into Bosdet's working methods and reveal the esteem in which he was held at the time. I am greatly indebted for these extracts to Mr Colin Dallison of Hexham who has done much research on the windows in the abbey.

"The design and execution of the east window has been entrusted to Mr H. T. Bosdet of Chiswick. The fact that the drawing and painting have been carried out in every detail by the artist himself, and the firing done under his personal supervision, has given to the execution of the windows a perfection and finish rarely met with. In the design of the scheme, we find the artist happily wedded to the craftsman." (1905)

"The artist is giving ungrudging thought, time and labour to the work, and there is abundant promise of noble execution. Mr Bosdet has furnished some of the richest colouring and a wondrous blending of colour. The work as a whole promises to establish his name in the North." (1905)

"The different lights of the window challenge attention by the interest and originality of the conception. The artist has refrained from overcrowding the glass and kept within the limitations imposed by his material. The glass has been selected with great care." (1905)

"His talented workmanship, rich scheme of colour and deep sense of reverence give the greatest satisfaction to us at Hexham" (1906)

"We have good reason to recognise the great artistic power of Mr Bosdet from the work he has already executed with so much satisfaction to those who have studied his work. He is very familiar with the architecture of the abbey and has carefully studied and watched the effects of its windows' light and shade. His work is thoroughly reverent in design, rich in those colours which harmonise with the abbey and perfect in draughtsmanship." (1907)

"Mr Bosdet does his own painting and being familiar with Hexham Abbey, tests his work by its surroundings, for he has a clear sense of the corporate relation existing between the parts of the building." (1916)

"The artist of the west window is Mr H. T. Bosdet who executed the east window in the choir. Right well has he executed his work. He has been entrusted with a great opportunity and he has been worthy of the trust. It has been a work of real devotion! This great west window is one of the largest and most important of all time in the North of England." (1918)

Henry Thomas Bosdet, age 50. Photograph taken at Trinity Manor in 1906 (detail)

Sites of Bosdet Stained Glass

● **Churches which hold Bosdet Stained Glass**

Bosdet's Jersey Windows

1898   St Helier's Church, Le Masurier Memorial Window,
The Annunciation.

1899   St Brelade's Church, James Remon Memorial Window,
The Nativity.
St Martin's Church, Le Bas Memorial Window, The Nativity.

1900   St Brelade's Church, Braithwaite Clerk Window,
The Good Shepherd.
St Brelade's Church, Le Quesne Window,
Christ after the Temptation.
St Brelade's Church, John Seale Window, The Annunciation.
St Brelade's Church, Martell Window, The Presentation in the
Temple and The Baptism of Christ by John the Baptist.
St Aubin on the Hill, The Wedding Feast at Cana.

1901   St Brelade's Church, John Norman Memorial Window,
The Crucifixion.
St Brelade's Church, The Falle Memorial Window,
The Sower and The Leavened Bread.
St Lawrence's Church, The Last Supper.

1903   St Mary's Church, Jean Collas Memorial Window,
The Presentation.

1905   St Saviour's Church, The Falle Memorial Window,
The Man of Sorrows and The Good Shepherd.

1907   St Martin's Church, The Aubin Memorial Window,
The Annunciation.
St Saviour's Church, John Fauvel Memorial, The Annunciation.
St Saviour's Church, St Martin of Tours.
St Saviour's Church, reredos, painted triptych behind altar.
St Aubin on the Hill, The Anne Marrett Memorial Window,
St Helier and St Magloire.

1908   St Martin's Church, The Aubin Memorial Window,
Sacrifice of Abraham.

1910   St John's Church, The Vaudin Memorial window, Two Archangels.

1911   St Brelade's Church, The Balleine Memorial Window,
       The Resurrection.

1912   St Ouen's Manor Chapel, The Legend of St Anne, six windows.

1914   Jersey Museum, Christ with St Peter and St Andrew, originally in
       East wall of Fishermen's Chapel. Moved to Museum in 1987.

1915   Jersey Museum, St Brelade preaching, originally from West wall of
       Fishermen's Chapel. Moved to Museum in 1987.
       Fishermen's Chapel, three small windows depicting the life of
       St Brelade. Although each has a brass memorial plaque dated
       1930, the designs and installation were approved by the
       Ecclesiastical Court on 26th January 1915.

1917   Gouray Church, The Whitley Memorial Window, Christ in
       Gethsemane.

1922   St Luke's Church, Rev Ralph Walker Memorial Window,
       The Good Shepherd.

1925   St John's Church, Valpy Memorial, The Resurrection.

1926   St John's Church, Nicolle Thanksgiving Window, The Lamb of God
       and St John. St Aubin on the Hill, Hamon/Weary Memorial
       Window, St Peter and The Good Shepherd.

Dates unknown

St Saviour's Church, Gibaut Memorial Window, The Light of the World and
The Bread of Life. Probably dates from early nineteen hundreds.

St Mary's Church, Clarence Collas Memorial Window, The Angels appear to
the Shepherds. Probably dates from the early nineteen hundreds.

St Mary's Church, John Collas/Jane Le Rossignol Memorial, The Adoration
of the Magi. Probably dates from the early years of the nineteen hundreds.

St Andrew's Church, The Ascension. This is a part of a Bosdet window
which was originally over the altar in St James' Church. It was transferred
to St Andrew's in 1984.

Holy Trinity, Mary Messervy Memorial Window, The Annunciation.

St Andrew's Church <small>(see map ref.2)</small>

Title   The Ascension of Christ

Position   North wall, towards the back of the church

Biblical Ref Acts I, verses 6 – 11

Memorial Inscription

In memory of Philip Edwin Jean, 5th June 1905 – 31st May 1984.
Peace Perfect Peace

Description

A window with three lights.

The central panel shows Christ in a deep red robe, ascending into Heaven,
with his right hand raised in blessing.

He is framed in a mandorla (Italian = almond), an almond-shaped halo
around the whole body which, in religious art, signifies a state of glory.

In the left panel, the Virgin Mary kneels with hands joined, looking up at her
departing Son. Two apostles stand behind her, one of them being James with
the brocade of his robe woven with his symbol, the scallop shell.

On the right are three more figures. The young man in the middle, holding
the book, represents St John the Beloved Disciple. The kneeling man with
hands joined is probably St Peter.

Historical note. The date on the memorial plaque is recent and is no
indication of the age of the window. The latter was originally in St James'
Church in St Helier and dates from the early part of the twentieth century.
When St James' was transformed into a concert hall, the window was
removed, reduced in height and installed in St Andrew's Church in 1984.

St Aubin on the Hill (1) (see map ref.14)

Title   The Wedding Feast at Cana

Position   West wall

Biblical Ref   John 2, verses 1 – 11

Signature   H. T. Bosdet 1900

Memorial Inscription

To the Glory of God and in Memory of George Balleine, born October 2nd
1809, died October 3rd 1898

St.Aubin on the Hill, St.Helier Window (detail)

Description

A very large window taking up much of the upper half of the west wall,
divided into four lights, surmounted by one large eight-lobed window, two
smaller six-lobed windows and one small roundel.

The wedding feast is depicted across the four panels, the whole being tied
together by the background architecture and by the long table which
stretches from side to side of the window.

The first panel, left, shows four apostles, looking inwards towards Christ in the second panel. Behind, servants are waiting at table, one of them carrying a peacock on a platter. Below, two angels hold a scroll bearing the words: "O ye angels of the Lord, bless ye the Lord."

In the second panel, Christ, seated, is blessing the water in three polychrome jars. Behind him stands an apostle and, in the background, there is the table with two guests. Below, two angels play stringed instruments. The third panel shows Mary addressing her son, with a servant kneeling beside her. In the background, bride and groom sit at table, surrounded by roses and goblets. Below, two angels play violas.

The fourth panel depicts two seated musicians with the steward of the feast standing nearby. The parents of the bride are in the background and a servant stands bearing a peacock fan. Below, two angels carry a scroll with the words "Praise Him and glorify Him forever." Above the four lights, the large lobed window shows an angel in a purple robe, seated on a rainbow, against a background of grapes and vine leaves, with the text: "Ye sun and moon, bless ye the Lord."

The small left-hand window shows another angel with red and blue wings holding the text: "O ye showers and dew, bless ye the Lord."

The right-hand window depicts a very striking angel with purple wings, wearing a yellow robe. The scroll bears the words: "O ye ice and snow, bless ye the Lord."

The small roundel at the heart of the whole window depicts a brilliant sun.

General observations.

A very rich composition in the Pre-Raphaelite manner, which gave Bosdet an opportunity to show off his talents as a draughtsman. It is notable for the balance of the design and the sumptuousness of the dress and the feast. The figures are superbly drawn, in particular the Virgin Mary, full of solicitude for her host and his guests. The garments and wings of the angels in the smaller windows are particularly vibrant. Their faces are exquisitely painted and the image of an angel seated on a rainbow in the top window is particularly striking. Arguably, this is the finest of Bosdet's larger windows in Jersey.

St Aubin on the Hill (2) *(see map ref.14)*

Title	a) St Helier b) St Magloire
Position	Chancel end of south wall
Signature	H. T. Bosdet, Grove Park Terrace, Chiswick, London. The Ecclesiastical Court minutes date this window 1907.

Memorial Inscription

A la Gloire de Dieu et en mémoire d'Anne Elizabeth Marrett, Dame du Franc Fief, née le 20 de mars 1822, décédée le 2 de novembre 1905.

(To the Glory of God and in memory of Anne Elizabeth Marrett, Dame of the Manor of Franc Fief, born 20th March 1822, died 2nd November 1905.)

St.Aubin on the Hill, The Wedding Feast at Cana (detail showing bride and groom)

Description

A double window with St Helier on the left and St Magloire on the right. Helier, bearded and in profile, wears a royal blue robe and holds a rod surmounted by a cross. On his belt hangs the hermit's water gourd. The background is a beautiful and intricate pattern of foliage in green, blue and white. The window bears the legend: " St Helerius, martyr, a Wandalis in hac insula occisus est" (St Helier, martyr, was killed in this Island by the Vandals).

Below, a smaller panel shows Helier asleep with his hand on the cross. A Vandal towers over him with sword raised high while, in the background, other Vandals wait near a dragon-headed boat with sail unfurled.

In the right-hand window, St Magloire stands full face, wearing episcopal vestments, with crozier in one hand and a small model of a church in the other (the symbol of a confessor, a saint who has not suffered martyrdom). The background is similar to the St Helier panel. The window bears the legend: "Sanctus Maglorius Episcopus et Confessor in hac insula mortuus est" (St Magloire, Bishop and Confessor, died in this Island).

The small panel below depicts the saint in white deacon's vestments, holding a wooden cross and preaching to the islanders. A boat rides the waves in the background. Above the two lights there is a small panel showing heraldic arms quartered with shells, horizontal bars and eagles' heads (armorial bearings of the Marrett family, cf Payne's Armorial of Jersey, page 275).

St.Aubin on the Hill,
The Wedding Feast at Cana (detail)

St Aubin (3) *(see map ref.14)*

Title	a) St Peter	b) The Good Shepherd

Position   South wall

Biblical Ref   a) Matthew 16, verses 13 – 19
                 b) John 10, verses 1 - 18

Signature

The minutes of the Ecclesiastical Court, dated 18th January 1926, attribute this window to Henry Thomas Bosdet.

Memorial Inscription

To the Glory of God and in loving memory of John Peter Hamon, Master Mariner and of Anne Weary, his wife, also of their children, Percy and Flora, this window is erected by their surviving children, Walter, Edith and Ella, AD 1926

Description

A window with two lights. The left light shows St Peter, holding a boat hook, standing in front of the mast and red sail of a boat. He is wearing a blue robe and a white and deep yellow cloak. Above him are the crossed keys, symbol of St Peter, and below a scroll bearing the words of Christ, "I will make you fishers of men" (Matthew 4, verse 19).

The light on the right represents the Good Shepherd. Jesus stands in white, blue and red robes, carrying a lamb on his right arm and holding a shepherd's crook in his left hand. Sheep graze in the background. Above him is a gold crown in a wreath of blue glass and, below, a scroll with the words, "I am the Good Shepherd" (John 10, verse 14).

Below each light are decorative panels of glass with stylised roses at their centre.

Above the two lights, in a small tri-lobed panel, an angel bears a scroll with the words which Jesus addressed to Peter, "Feed my sheep" (John 21, verse 17).

St Brelade (1) *(see map ref.13)*

Title	Christ after the Temptation
Position	First window in south wall, on the right as you enter
Biblical Ref	Matthew 4, verse 11
Signature	H.T. Bosdet, Grove Park Terrace, Chiswick 1900

Memorial Inscription

To the Glory of God and in loving memory of Amelia Le Quesne, wife of Alfred Le Gallais, born Nov 5th 1842, died Feb 10th 1894.

This window is erected by her three daughters, Mary Hargraves, Maud Davis, Evelyn Goddard.

Description   A single panel.

Christ is shown kneeling and in profile, after his temptation and forty days in the desert. Angels in priestly robes are ministering to him, one carrying a chalice. The towers and walls of Jerusalem rise in the background and, to the right, a distant ship ploughs through the sea, under full sail.

Above, there is a crown of thorns with the biblical quotation: "And angels came and ministered unto him".

Below the memorial inscription appear symbols of Christ's temptation: a bag of gold coins, a sceptre and a crown.

St.Helier's Church, Annunciation Window (detail)

St Brelade (2) ^(see map ref.13)

Title   The Crucifixion

Position   South wall, second window on the right as you enter

Biblical Ref   Mark 15, verses 33-41
                 John 19, verses 25-37

Signature   H.T. Bosdet, Inglewood, Grove Park, Chiswick, London

Memorial Inscription

Cette fenêtre est présentée par Elizabeth Mary Norman, en mémoire de son père, John Norman, fils Jacques 1901.

(This window was donated by Elizabeth Mary Norman, in memory of her father, John Norman, son of James 1901.)

Description

A single panel.

Christ hangs dying on the cross. His mother Mary stands on the left and John the Beloved Disciple on the right, representing the moment when Christ entrusted his mother and St John to each other's care.

Mary Magdalen is at the foot of the cross, wrapping her hair around Christ's feet, recalling the earlier incident when she washed the feet of Christ and dried them with her hair.

Soldiers and public stand in the background and the buildings of Jerusalem can be seen in the distance. Four small angels hover above the cross, with the dove of the Holy Ghost above them. To the right of Christ, a Roman soldier holds a banner with the words: "Véritablement, cet homme était le fils de Dieu" (Truly, this man was the Son of God).

St Brelade (3) *(see map ref.13)*

Title   a) The Sower   b) The Leavened Yeast

Position   South wall, third window on right as you enter

Biblical Ref   Matthew 13, verses 4 – 23 and verse 33

Signature   H. T. Bosdet 1901

Memorial Inscription

"To the Glory of God and in Memory of Edward Falle MA, Rector of this Parish from 1829 to 1882, died 1899, and of Carterette Le Couteur, his wife, died 1890, our Father and Mother."

Description

a) In the right-hand panel, against a background of stylised trees, a sower strides out, holding a basket of seed in his left hand and scattering with his right. He wears a red tunic with a pattern of oak leaves and acorns and on his feet he has Roman calf boots. Foxgloves and thistles grow on either side of him.

b) In the left-hand panel, a woman, wearing a deep indigo dress and richly embroidered cloak, carries a loaf of leavened dough on a small wooden platter. Her finely drawn head is accentuated by the wooden window frame which surrounds it.

Both figures are surmounted by canopies of Gothic stonework and white and gold stylised foliage.

Three small panels above show an angel bearing a book entitled "The Word of God" and two scrolls with quotations from the Scriptures: "A sower went out to sow" and "Till the whole was leavened".

The two figures almost fill the window frames which contain them. They are profoundly spiritual, the sower striding out with resolution, symbolising the spreading of God's word, and the woman, bearing the bread as an offering, a token of her wifely and maternal vocation.

St Brelade (4) *(see map ref.13)*

Title   The Good Shepherd

Position   South wall, in the chancel

Biblical Ref   John 10, verses 1 – 18 Psalm 23

Signature   H. T. Bosdet 1900

Memorial Inscription

No inscription in the window design but a brass plaque beneath it bears the name of William Braithwaite Clerk MA, Vicar of Alne, Yorkshire.

Description

A double window.

On the left, Christ stands in profile, holding a shepherd's crook, with the quotation from Psalm 23 "He leadeth me beside the still waters".

On the right, a very striking Christ, in deep magenta robe, releases the sheep caught in the brambles, with the quotation "He seeketh that which is gone astray" (Matthew 18, verse 12).

The panels are surmounted by two angels, one bearing a crown of thorns and the other a royal crown of life. They are surrounded by stylised blackberry blossom and fruit, mostly in white and gold. Higher still, there are three small panels of briar roses, with flowers and hips.

St Brelade (5) (see map ref.13)

Title   The Resurrection

Position   North wall

Biblical Ref   Matthew 28, verses 1 – 7

Signature   H. T. Bosdet

Memorial Inscription

A la Gloire de Dieu et en Mémoire de nos Parents John Balleine et Adelaide, née Arthur, et d'Adelina, notre soeur. Cette fenêtre est érigée par le Revd. John Arthur Balleine, Recteur de cette Paroisse, et par ses frères et soeur, Arthur Edwin, Ernest Orange et Florence Elizabeth, 1911.

(To the Glory of God and in Memory of our parents John Balleine and Adelaide, née Arthur, and of Adelina, our sister. This window is erected by the Reverend John Arthur Balleine, Rector of this Parish, and by his brothers and sister, Arthur Edwin, Ernest Orange and Florence Elizabeth, 1911.)

Description

A double window.

In the left panel, Christ rises from the tomb, with three Roman soldiers sleeping nearby. In the open tomb can be seen the folded shroud and Christ's crown of thorns. In the right panel, an angel bearing a palm of victory, addresses the three Marys.

Mary Magdalen kneels with an amphora of oil which she had brought to anoint Christ's dead body. She is often identified by the amphora of oil, which recalls the earlier occasion when she washed and anointed Christ's feet.

The background shows a small area of Jerusalem.

Above, a window shows a bust of Christ, crowned and holding a sceptre, with the text: "Bienheureux les morts qui meurent au Seigneur" (Blessed are the dead who die in the Lord).

St Brelade (6) *(see map ref.13)*

Title   The Annunciation

Position   Middle of North Wall

Biblical Ref   Luke 1, verses 26 – 38

Signature   H. T. Bosdet 1900

Memorial Inscription

Cette fenêtre est présentée par John Alfred Seale, Connétable lors de la restauration de cette église, 1900.

(This window was presented by John Alfred Seale, Constable during the restoration of this church 1900.)

Description

A double window.

On the left, the Archangel Gabriel, holding the lily, symbol of purity and virginity, addresses Mary. Five smaller angels look on, holding a scroll with the words: "Hail thou that art highly favoured."

On the right, Mary sits before a lectern bearing an open book showing the text: "For unto us a child is born, unto us a son is given." The lectern is surmounted by a lantern and four small angels bearing a gold crown and the text: "Behold the handmaid of the Lord."

Above, a small panel with armorial bearings of a star, four wolves' heads and the motto: "In caelo salus" (Salvation in Heaven). Arms of the Seale Family (cf. Payne's Armorial of Jersey, page 330).

Opposite: St.Aubin on the Hill,
St.Magloire window (detail)

St Brelade (7) *(see map ref.13)*

Title	The Nativity
Position	North wall, near the rear of church
Biblical Ref	Luke 2, verses 1 – 20
Signature	H. T. Bosdet 1899

Memorial Inscription

To the Glory of God and in loving memory of James Remon, died August 19th 1859 and of Anne Marett, his wife, died November 25th 1869.

Erected by their son James Marett and their daughters Sophia and Susan Pipon.

Description

A single panel.

In the foreground, Mary presents her baby to the world. Joseph stands behind, leaning on his lily staff, accompanied by three angels. To the left, three shepherds look on, one of them playing a pipe. Nearby, a large star announces the arrival of the Wise Men. Three cows stand on the right and doves perch on the roof of the stable. The whole composition is surrounded by a frame of stylised vegetation.

St Brelade (8) (see map ref.13)

Title   a) The Presentation in the Temple
                             b) The Baptism of Christ

Position   High in the west wall

Biblical Ref   a) Luke 2, verses 22 – 38
                             b) Matthew 3, verses 13 - 17

Memorial Inscription

Ces vitraux sont offerts par Edouard Martell de Cognac en souvenir du berceau de sa famille, mai 1900. (These stained glass windows are presented by Edouard Martell of Cognac in memory of the birthplace of his family, May 1900.)

Description

A window with two lights.

The left panel represents the Presentation of the Child Jesus in the Temple. Simeon cradles the child in his arms with Mary and Joseph kneeling in front of him. Joseph is holding a small cage containing two doves, a thanksgiving offering to the Temple. An angel stands behind Simeon, with outstretched wings.

The right panel portrays the Baptism of Christ by John the Baptist. Jesus, in a deep red garment, stands in the waters of the Jordan and John, from the bank, pours water on Jesus' head. John holds a staff crowned with a long scroll, inscribed with the words "Ecce Agnus Dei" (Behold the Lamb of God). A second angel stands near John and a fruiting orange tree grows in the background.

Both lights are surmounted by fully blown pink roses and the whole is capped by a red heraldic shield bearing three gilt hammers, the arms of the Martell family.

St Brelade (9) *(see map ref.13)*

Title St Brelade en Voyage (The Journey of St Brelade).

Position Fishermen's Chapel, North wall

Signature

No signature. The date on the memorial inscription is misleading; the designs for the three small windows in the Fishermen's Chapel were approved by the Ecclesiastical Court in 1915.

Memorial Inscription

Don de Walter Francis Hamon de St Aubin, en mémoire de ses ancêtres, Branche Weary, A.D.1930 (The gift of Walter Francis Hamon of St Aubin, in memory of his ancestors, Weary Branch, A.D.1930)

Description

St Brelade stands in prayer in the prow of a vessel, sailing out of the frame towards the spectator. The figure-head of the ship is a large crucifix. The saint is surrounded by six companions, one holding an oar as a tiller and another hanging onto the rigging. The ship ploughs through turbulent aquamarine seas. The picture is bordered by a decorated stone Norman arch.

The composition is animated, the faces expressive and the colours rich and harmonious.

The legend of St Brelade has much in common with the story of St Brendan the Voyager (circa 486 – 578AD) whose journeys are recounted in the tenth century tale "Brendan's Voyage" (cf.The Penguin Dictionary of Saints, 1965).

St Brelade (10) *(see map ref.13)*

Title   St Brelade saying Mass

Position   Fishermen's Chapel, South wall by the altar

Signature   Refer back to St Brelade (9).

Memorial Inscription

Don d'Edward Le Bas de Londres en mémoire du berceau de sa famille
A.D.1930

(Gift of Edward Le Bas of London in memory of the birthplace of his family
A.D. 1930)

Description

St Brelade, in a bright red cloak, says Mass and blesses the chalice, before
an altar covered with a white altar cloth and bearing a silver paten. Five
elderly men kneel in prayer. Above the group and also at the feet of the
worshippers there are numerous birds, painted in grisaille (grey
monochrome). The whole is bordered by a Norman arch.

Opposite: St.Brelade's Church,
Fishermen's Chapel, The Journey
of St.Brelade (detail)

Overleaf: St.John's Church,
Resurrection window (detail)

St Brelade (11) *(see map ref.13)*

Title   La Jeunesse de St Brelade (St Brelade's Youth)

Position   Fishermen's Chapel, middle of south wall

Signature   Refer back to St Brelade (9)

Memorial Inscription

Don de John Edward Le Boutillier, Juré Justicier, en mémoire des membres décédés de sa famille A.D. 1930.

(Gift of John Edward Le Boutillier, Jurat of the Royal Court, in memory of the deceased members of his family A.D. 1930.)

Description

St Brelade is seated in profile with a big volume on the desk before him. The floor of the room is tiled and the sea and sky can be seen through the small window in the background. In front of St Brelade, an elderly saint blesses and instructs him. This person is wearing a pallium, a white woollen stole embroidered with black crosses, which usually denotes an archbishop. The picture is framed by a Norman arch.

Jersey Museum, History of Jersey (see map ref.6)

Title	a) St Brelade preaching
	b) Christ with St Peter and St Andrew
Position	In the Religious Section of Our Island Story
Signature	H. T. Bosdet

According to the minutes of the Ecclesiastical Court, the window of Christ and two apostles dates from 1914, and that of St Brelade from 1915.

Memorial Inscription

A la Gloire de Dieu et en mémoire de Peter Briard, Lieut. Bailli, décédé le 25 mars 1906, âgé de 76 ans. Ces vitraux sont présentés par sa veuve Marie Richardson, née Tardiff.

(To the Glory of God and in memory of Peter Briard, Lieut. Bailiff, died 25th March 1906, aged 76 years. These stained glass windows were presented by his widow Mary Richardson, née Tardiff.)

Description

These two windows, framed in separate metal surrounds, were originally in the Fishermen's Chapel, St Brelade. Their general condition is poor and they were removed to greater safety in 1987, when the Chapel was excavated and restored.

The left-hand window, originally in the west wall of the Fishermen's Chapel, is slightly taller than the other, and shows St Brelade in priestly robes, standing on seaweed on the shore and holding a staff topped by a crucifix in his right hand. In front of him kneels a local chief, indicated by a plain gold band around his head, and his followers, all being blessed by the saint. In the background, there is the rust coloured sail of a boat and cliffs in the distance.

The right-hand window, from the east end of the Chapel, depicts Christ with arms outstretched. Below him, in two smaller panels, stand St Peter with his symbolic keys and St Andrew supporting his traditional diagonal cross. Below them is a scroll bearing the words: "Erant enim Piscatores" (For they were Fishermen).

Gouray *(see map ref. 7)*

Title   Christ's Agony in the Garden of Gethsemane

Position   South wall

Biblical Ref   Luke 22, verses 39-53

Signature   H. T. Bosdet 1917

Memorial Inscription

To the Glory of God, this window is placed by Elias George Whitley in loving memory of his father and mother, Elias Whitley died 1859 and Elizabeth Whitley died 1914.

Description

A single lancet, over twelve feet high.

From above, the dove of the Holy Ghost hovers over the scene. Below, an angel in priestly robes bears a chalice down to the distressed figure of Christ.

In the main part of the window, Christ kneels under a canopy of trees. He is shown in profile, head bowed with hands joined tightly on his lap. The curve of his body reveals his inner desolation and grief. Behind him rise the towers and walls of Jerusalem and through the bushes soldiers approach to apprehend him. Beneath Christ are the words of his prayer: "Not my will but Thine be done."

The surrounding space is filled with stylised foliage and berries.

St Helier *(see map ref.4)*

Title   The Annunciation

Position   North wall of west porch

Biblical Ref   Luke 1, verses 26-38

Signature   H.T. Bosdet 1898

Memorial Inscription

To the Glory of God and in loving memory of John Le Masurier died August 13th 1896. Erected by his widow.

Description

A double window.

The left-hand light shows the Archangel Gabriel in profile, standing on a cloud beneath an architectural canopy and holding a Madonna lily in his left hand.

The right-hand light depicts the Virgin Mary in three-quarter profile with spinning wheel and distaff. The distaff is a stick which holds a quantity of wool or flax from which thread is spun. It symbolises the domestic role of women and was a common attribute of the Virgin Mary in medieval representations of the Annunciation.

Mary sits beneath a Gothic canopy, hands clasped above her left breast. The dove of the Holy Ghost hovers above her head.

Beneath Mary's feet is a rich carpet and on the sill near her head stands a bowl of roses. Lower down, two angels carry scrolls bearing the memorial inscription to John Le Masurier. This is a particularly rich and balanced composition which was originally in the vestry but was moved to its present position in 1975.

Holy Trinity *(see map ref.9)*

Title   The Annunciation

Position   South wall of chancel

Biblical Ref   Luke 1, verses 26 to 38.

Memorial Inscription

A la mémoire de Mary de Gruchy, épouse d'Alfred Messervy, décédée le 18 septembre 1887 âgée de 32 ans.

(In memory of Mary de Gruchy, wife of Alfred Messervy, died 18th September 1887, aged 32 years.)

Description

A double window.

The left light shows the Archangel Gabriel, dressed in priestly robes, standing on a pale blue cloud. He holds a lily in his left hand and his right hand is raised in greeting.

In the right-hand light, the Virgin Mary kneels in profile, with hands joined. Behind her is a book on a lectern and the curtains and cushions of a bed.

Both figures are surmounted by canopies of Gothic stonework.

The dove, symbol of the Holy Spirit, hovers above. Scrolls below the figures bear the words: " Tu es bénie entre les femmes" and "Voici la servante du Seigneur" ("You are blessed among women" and "Behold the handmaid of the Lord").

Holy Trinity, Annunciation window (detail)

Overleaf: St.Martin's Church, Nativity window (detail)

St John (1) *(see map ref.10)*

Title   Two Angels

Position   South wall, in chancel

Signature   H. T. Bosdet 1910

Memorial Inscription

To the Glory of God and in Memory of John Arthur Vaudin and of Mary Ann Pinel, his wife, who died in 1884.

This window is presented by their son, John Pinel Vaudin.

Description

A double window with a smaller window above.

The left-hand light depicts the Archangel Gabriel holding his symbolic lily. Above his head is a scroll bearing the words: "Holy, Holy, Holy." On the right, the Archangel Michael stands in full armour, holding a spear in his left hand. He wears a fine gold coronet around his hair and holds an orb in his right hand. Above him are the words: "Lord God of Hosts." The dove flies above, symbol of the Holy Spirit.

St John (2) *(see map ref.10)*

Title	The Resurrection
Position	North wall, in the choir
Biblical Ref	Matthew 28, verses 1 to 7

Signature

The Ecclesiastical Court delivered a faculty for the installation of this window in 1925. The minutes mention that the window was designed by H. T. Bosdet.

Memorial Inscription

Ce vitrail est érigé à la Gloire de Dieu et à la mémoire de la Famille Valpy de cette Paroisse, par Clara Valpy.

(This window is donated by Clara Valpy to the Glory of God and in Memory of the Valpy Family of this Parish.)

Description

A large window of three lights, with three smaller windows above.

In the centre panel, Christ rises from the tomb in glory. Around His feet, the Roman soldiers are still sleeping. Above His head are Christ's own words: "I am the Resurrection and the Life."

In the left-hand light, Christ blesses Mary Magdalen who is kneeling before Him. He carries a staff from which flutters a pennant marked with a cross in red. The towers and buildings of Jerusalem rise in the background. The scroll above His head reads: "I ascend unto my Father and your Father."

The right-hand light shows the angel greeting the Three Marys. His garments are white and he carries the palm of victory. Mary Magdalen kneels before him, with her jar of oil. Behind her, the Virgin Mary stands in profile, looking at the angel, hands clasped on her breast. Behind her again, there is just a glimpse of the third Mary. The words of the angel appear above in a scroll: "He is not here, He is risen."

The small panels above show Christ the King and two angels in adoration.

This window is particularly remarkable for its vibrant colour contrasts and for the Pre-Raphaelite depiction of Mary Magdalen in the right-hand light. The Risen Christ and the Roman soldiers in the centre panel strongly resemble the same figures in the St Brelade's Church Resurrection window.

St.Helier's Church, Annunciation Window, The Angel Gabriel (detail)

St John (3) *(see map ref.10)*

Title   a) The Lamb of God
                  b) St John the Baptist

Position   South wall, near font

Biblical Ref   John 1, verse 29

Signature

No signature. The Ecclesiastical Court granted a faculty for the installation of this window in 1926. H. T. Bosdet is mentioned in the minutes.

Memorial Inscription

To the Glory of God and as a thanks offering from the Reverend E St John Nicolle BD, Rector of this Parish during 34 years and from his wife, Ada Le Boutillier, 1926.

Description

A double window.

The left-hand light depicts Christ, crowned with thorns and holding a reed in his hands, which are tied with a rope. The scroll says: "Behold the Lamb of God."

On the right, St John the Baptist stands holding a wooden staff topped with a cross. He looks across to Christ and points Him out with his right hand. Above him are the words: "Which taketh away the sins of the world."

The two figures are placed against a deep green curtain edged with gold braid. Their heads and haloes are surrounded by areas of clear glass which is unusual in a Bosdet window.

Above the two lights, there is a small panel of glass depicting a golden chalice, surrounded by a scroll bearing the words: "The Blood of the Lamb."

St Lawrence (1) *(see map ref.1)*

Title   The Last Supper

Position   Filling the east gable, behind the high altar

Biblical Ref   Mark 14, verses 17-25

Signature   H.T. Bosdet, Inglewood, Grove Park Terrace, Chiswick.

Memorial Inscription

Ad majorem Dei gloriam AD 1901

(To the greater glory of God AD 1901)

Description

A very large window of four lights, surmounted by ten smaller panels. A long horizontal table, covered by a white embroidered cloth, ties the four lights together. It bears a plate of fruit, three other gold plates and a chalice.

Christ stands with six of the apostles, the other six being seated. His head is very sensitively painted, showing strain and suffering. One hand holds the bread and the other is raised in blessing. Judas, in the group on Christ's right, is distinguishable by his sombre halo and the leather money-bag in front of him. Peter, on the left of Jesus, grasps the hilt of the sword which he will later use in a vain attempt to defend his master in the Garden of Gethsemane (John 18, verses 10 & 11).

The background is formed entirely of flamboyant Gothic architecture.

The smaller panels above show angels, each bearing a different symbol of Christ's Passion. At the very summit of the group is an angel bearing a shield showing Christ's monogram IHS (Jesus Hominum Salvator, Jesus Saviour of Mankind). On either side of him, two very small panels contain scrolls with the words: "By Thy cross and passion, good Lord deliver us."

In the middle row, the left-hand angel, with mauve wings, bears a shield decorated with rope, the spear which pierced Christ's side and the sponge on the end of a rod which was used to quench His thirst. The angel on the right holds the thirty pieces of silver which were Judas' reward for his

betrayal of Christ. In the bottom row of small panels, the left-hand angel, with pink and green wings, holds a shield showing the crown of thorns and the three nails of Christ's crucifixion.

The middle angel, with brilliant orange and red wings, supports a book which shows the first and last letters of the Greek alphabet, Alpha and Omega, the Beginning and the End. The angel on the right, with purple wings, holds a crown of glory. The heads and haloes of each of the angels are framed by their wings which almost join over each head. Above each one is a small rotating star and in the last two small panels on either side is a brilliant star on a blue ground.

The complete window must be one of Bosdet's finest for the subtleties of its colours, the fine drawing, the balance of the composition and the reverence of its atmosphere.

St Lawrence (2) *(see map ref.1)*

Title	a) Christ the Light of the World
	b) The Good Shepherd.

Position   Middle of North wall

Biblical Ref   a) John 8, verse 12
b) John 10, verses 1 – 18

Signature

The minutes of the Ecclesiastical Court show that a faculty for the installation of this window was granted 9th April 1923.

Memorial Inscription

Erigé à la mémoire d'Elizabeth Valpy, veuve de James Le Couteur, décédée le 1er mars 1918, par Clara Valpy sa soeur.

(Erected in memory of Elizabeth Valpy, widow of James Le Couteur, died 1st March 1918, by Clara Valpy, her sister.)

Description

A large double window.

On the left, Christ, crowned with thorns and carrying a lantern, is depicted as the Light of the World. He stands among flowers against a background of dark trees and blue sky. On the right, Christ is portrayed as the Good Shepherd. He cradles a lamb on his left arm and holds a shepherd's crook in his right hand. He is surrounded on either side by sheep which are partly concealed by the greenery. Both figures are framed by borders of stylised Gothic foliage.

Above, in a smaller panel, an angel displays a scroll bearing the quotation: "The Son of Man is come to seek and to save that which was lost" (Luke 19 verse 10).

Previous Page: St.Lawrence's Church, Last Supper Window (detail)

Opposite: St.Lawrence's Church, Cartoon of Christ from The Last Supper (detail)

St Martin (1) (see map ref.8)

Title   The Annunciation

Position   North wall by the pulpit

Biblical Ref   Luke 1, verses 26-38

Signature   H. T. Bosdet Chiswick June 1907

Memorial Inscription

To the Glory of God this window is erected by Jane Aubin in memory of George Aubin her husband.

Description

A double window.

In the left-hand panel, the Virgin Mary sits in profile, her joined hands resting on a book on her lap. She is wearing a deep blue cloak, a colour which was often, and still is, associated with the Virgin Mary. In medieval times, it was made from the mineral lapis lazuli, the great cost of which was a measure of the devotion of the person commissioning the work.

Mary sits in a garden, with cobbles beneath her feet. An arcaded wall, revealing blue sky, forms the background. Lilies and climbing roses grow beside her. The Holy Ghost, in the traditional form of a dove, faces Mary in profile.

The right panel shows the archangel Gabriel in profile, wearing a deep red cloak and a sage green gown. He stands on a cloud, with right hand raised in greeting and a lily in his left hand.

Both figures are beneath canopies of Gothic architecture.

Above is a smaller, central light showing Sarah, Abraham's wife, holding a scroll with the promise which God made to Abraham: "She shall be the Mother of Nations" (Genesis 17, verse 16).

St Martin (2) *(see map ref.8)*

Title	The Nativity
Position	East wall, in the south chancel
Biblical Ref	Luke 2, verses 1-20
Signature	H. T. Bosdet 1899

Memorial Inscription

To the Glory of God and in affectionate memory of Eleonore Mary Emily Nicolle, wife of Charles Godfray Le Bas. This window is erected by her loving husband.

Description

A window composed of three lights, and nine smaller panels.

Left-hand light. Against a background of a wooden stable and decorated architectural borders, the Three Kings present their gifts, one standing and two kneeling.

The centre light shows Joseph leaning on his lily staff, looking straight out of the picture. To his left, the bright star of the East shines over the cattle.

Mary, seated on a stool, looks down at her baby, her hands clasped in wonderment. The child lies on straw and holds his hands up to his mother. In the right-hand light, three shepherds worship the Christ Child, one standing with a crook and the others kneeling.

Above the main panels, there are six small decorative panels and three larger panels showing the heads of bearded prophets, identified respectively as Daniel, Isaiah and Jeremiah.

The composition of this window is particularly beautiful. All the figures combine to form a circle around the central figure of the Virgin Mary looking down at her new-born child.

St Martin (3) *(see map ref.8)*

Title	Abraham's Sacrifice
Position	Middle of south wall
Biblical Ref	Genesis 22, verses 1-19
Signature	H. T. Bosdet, Inglewood, Grove Park Terrace, Chiswick

Memorial Inscription

To the Glory of God, this window is dedicated by Jane Aubin, widow of the late George Aubin Esq., of George St., Hanover Sq., London and St Mark's Road, Jersey, March 1908.

Description

A double window.

In the left-hand light, Abraham, in profile, raises a dagger in his right hand, in obedience to God's command to sacrifice his son Isaac. In the thicket at his feet, a ram is caught in the brambles.

In the right-hand panel, Isaac lies on a sacrificial pyre, hands and feet bound. Above him, an angel stays Abraham's hand and places a protecting hand on Isaac's head.

Above, a smaller panel shows an angel holding the text: "Thou hast not withheld thine only son from Me" (Genesis 22, verse 12).

As with so many Old Testament stories which are precursors of events in the New Testament, Abraham's sacrifice of his son Isaac in the Old Testament foreshadows God's sacrifice of his son Jesus in the New Testament. Isaac bound to the pyre brings to mind Christ nailed to the cross.

Interesting footnote. A receipt, signed by Henry Thomas Bosdet and dated 1st April 1908, shows that the cost of this window, including packing, insurance, installation in the church and external wire guards was £90.

St Mary (1) *(see map ref.11)*

Title   The Presentation in the Temple

Position   South wall, above the chancel altar rail

Biblical Ref   Luke 2, verses 21-35

Signature   H.T. Bosdet, Xmas 1903 (? – date not entirely legible.)

Memorial Inscription

A la Gloire de Dieu et en mémoire de Jean Collas 1794-1872, Carterette Vibert, son épouse, 1800-1864, Jeanne Vibert née Dumaresque, mère de la susdite 1776-1861. (To the Glory of God and in memory of John Collas, Carterette Vibert his wife and Jeanne Vibert née Dumaresque, her mother.)

Description

A double panel.

The window represents the bringing of the infant Jesus by his parents to the Temple in Jerusalem to be consecrated to God, in keeping with Jewish law and custom. The rite required the offering of a pair of turtle-doves. Joseph stands twirling his moustache and holding in his right hand a small wicker cage containing the doves. Mary kneels in profile, hands crossed over her breast.

Simeon holds the child Jesus on his right arm and intones his great prayer: "Lord, dismiss now Thy servant in peace, for mine eyes have seen Thy salvation which Thou hast prepared before the face of all people, a light to lighten the Gentiles and the glory of Thy people Israel".

The figures are surmounted by stone canopies with scrolls showing the opening line of Simeon's prayer: "Seigneur, tu laisses aller ton serviteur maintenant en paix, car mes yeux ont vu ton salut" (Lord, dismiss now Thy servant in peace, for mine eyes have seen Thy salvation).

Above, a small cruciform window shows the bust of an angel carrying an open book inscribed: "La Parole de Dieu" (The Word of God).

St Mary (2) *(see map ref.8)*

Title   The Adoration of the Magi

Position   South wall, in the choir

Biblical Ref   Matthew 2, verses 1-12

Memorial Inscription

A la gloire de Dieu et en mémoire de John Collas 1825-1899, Jane Le Rossignol 1831-1894. Ce vitrail est érigé par leurs enfants.

(To the glory of God and in memory of John Collas 1825-1899 and Jane Le Rossignol 1831-1894. This stained glass window was donated by their children.)

Description

Two panels.

The left panel represents the Holy Family. Against a timber stable background, with ox and ass, Joseph stands holding his lily staff. Mary is seated with Jesus on her lap. The right panel shows the Three Kings in adoration, one kneeling in profile bearing a gold crown.

Above both panels there is elaborate Gothic architecture with the text: "Je t'ai donné pour être la lumière des nations" (I gave you to be the light of the nations). High above, a small cruciform window depicts the bust of an angel holding a five-pointed star.

St Mary (3) *(see map ref.8)*

Title	The Angels appear to the Shepherds
Position	South wall, near the pulpit
Biblical Ref	Luke 2, verses 8-20

Memorial Inscription

A la gloire de Dieu et en mémoire de Clarence Hardeley Collas 1858-1881, Adolphus Collas 1868-1874. Erigé par leurs frères et leurs soeurs.

(To the Glory of God and in memory of Clarence Hardeley Collas 1858-1881 and Adolphus Collas 1868-1874. Donated by their brothers and sisters.)

Description

A double window. On the left, the shepherds hear the greeting of the Angel and, on the right, the Angel tells the shepherds of the birth of the Christ Child. Above their heads there are canopies of Gothic architecture with a scroll bearing the words: "Paix sur la terre, bonne volonté envers les hommes" (Peace on earth, goodwill to all men). This window is notable for its dark, rich colours and finely drawn faces and hands. Above, in a small cruciform window, an angel holds the text: "Gloire soit à Dieu" (Glory be to God).

St Ouen's Manor Chapel (1) (see map ref.12)

Title   The Saviour and St Anne

Position   East wall, behind the altar

Description

A single window in a Norman arch, depicting Christ the Saviour holding a chalice and St Anne, mother of the Virgin Mary, turned towards her grandson with hands joined in prayer. Her head is beautifully drawn and her robes are in a striking combination of apple green and dark blue.

The head of each figure is surrounded by medallions with identifying initials: S for St Sauveur (St Saviour) and A for St Anne. Above them is the half figure of the prophet Zephaniah, wearing a crown of yellow leaves and holding a long scroll bearing words from his own writings: "Réjouis-toi, égaye-toi de tout ton coeur, fille de Jerusalem", Sophonie 3, 14, (Be glad and rejoice with all thy heart, O daughter of Jerusalem. Zephaniah 3, verse 14).

The Manor Chapel is dedicated to St Anne and the six windows in the chapel portray scenes from her life. What we know about the life of Anne and her husband Joachim comes from the Protoevangelium of St James the Less, an early writing which is not part of the Bible and is therefore considered as legend.

St Anne is particularly venerated and loved in Brittany and she is the patron saint of that part of France. Her great shrine is at Auray and her feast day is 26th July. Her help is particularly solicited by childless couples and by young women in search of a husband.

Previous pages: St.Helier's Church,
Annunciation window (detail)

Opposite: St.Ouen's Manor Chapel,
The Angel appears to Anne (detail)

St Ouen's Manor Chapel (2) *(see map ref.12)*

Title   St Anne weeping in the garden

Position   North wall, to the left of the altar

Description

A small rectangular window.

St Anne is seated on a formal stone throne, classical in its simplicity. The stone is pale green and the back of the chair, in cream stone, rises up to frame the saint's head and rich red halo. Stylised trees behind her and a paved foreground indicate a garden.

St Anne is disconsolate because of her childless state, her eyes are downcast and her hands joined together on one side of her lap. Her robe is deep red, a colour often used to symbolise love and the green of her brocade cloak, patterned with the Gothic letter A, symbolises spring, rebirth and hope. Beneath are the words: "Ste Anne pleure dans le jardin" (Saint Anne weeps in the garden).

This is a restrained composition in tones of red and green, with touches of turquoise and blue. The whole is framed in a delicate border of golden foliage.

St Ouen's Manor Chapel (3) (see map ref.12)

Title   Joachim rejected by the High Priest

Position   Middle of North wall, on left as you enter

Signature   H. T. Bosdet 1912

Description

A small, narrow window in a rounded arch.

In the foreground, Joachim, Anne's husband, comes to the Temple bearing his offering of a lamb. Behind him, to the right, St Anne waits, her hands joined in prayer.

Above them, towers the High Priest wearing the breastplate with twelve precious stones, each representing one of the twelve tribes of Israel. With him stand other characters in medieval costume and a woman bearing a lidded dish in gold. The High Priest's look is severe and his left hand is raised in dismissal. Behind the group, Jerusalem is represented by a large classical archway.

According to the legend of St Anne, her husband's offering at the Temple was rejected by the priest because, after many years of marriage, Joachim had fathered no children for the nation of Israel and was therefore considered unworthy. Joachim fled in shame to the desert where he prayed and fasted for forty days and nights. For her part, Anne hid away ashamed, reproaching herself for her childlessness and anxious about her beloved Joachim.

Opposite: Gouray Church, Jesus in the Garden of Gethsemane, (decorative detail)

St Ouen's Manor Chapel (4) *(see map ref.12)*

Title   The Angel appears to St Anne

Position   South wall, to the right of the altar

Signature   H. T. Bosdet 1912

Description

A narrow window in a round arched aperture.

St Anne, in a richly decorated cloak with dark blue lining and an olive green dress, listens to the reassuring message of the angel who, according to the legend of St Anne, is telling her that she will have a child to be named Mary. The angel, floating on a cloud, has bright red wings and his hand is raised in greeting.

Behind them, conifers fill the skyline and roses grow in profusion around Anne and the angel. The space above is filled with a decorative panel of delicate arabesques of foliage.

St Ouen's Manor Chapel (5) *(see map ref.12)*

Title   The Angel appears to Joachim

Position   High in the west wall

Description

A window of two narrow lights in rounded arches.

In the left-hand panel, an angel with bright red wings bears a scroll with the words: "In nomine Dei altissimi" (In the name of the most high God). He tells Joachim to leave his flocks and return to the Golden Gate of the Temple where he will meet his wife Anne. He reassures Joachim that his childless days are over and that Anne will conceive a child.

Beneath the angel, in a small and delightful cameo on the left, Joachim is shown resting among his sheep, in a sylvan setting of rocks, bushes and foxgloves.

In the right panel, against a background of trees and blue sky, Joachim raises his hands to the angel in wonderment and gratitude.

Above each figure is a panel of arabesques of foliage.

In the lower part of each light are two smaller panels, the first showing King David playing his harp and the second depicting Abraham holding a scroll of parchment.

St.Andrew's Church,
The Ascension window (detail)

St Ouen's Manor Chapel (6) *(see map ref.12)*

Title   St Anne and Joachim meet at the Golden Gate

Position   South wall, to the right on entry

Signature   H. T. Bosdet 1912

Description

Joachim and St Anne follow the instructions given to them by the angels and they meet and embrace at the Golden Gate of the Temple. After their shame and distress at being childless, their joy is abundant. Both are in highly decorated grisaille (grey monochrome) robes with sleeves and lining in rich reds, blues and greens. Three women accompany St Anne and three of his fellow-shepherds stand behind Joachim. In the background is the Golden Gate, an ornate Roman arch with gilded carvings, and the towers of several buildings, symbolising Jerusalem. Above the figures is the decorative panel of foliage common to all the four narrow windows in the series, but this one is rendered dramatic by the deep red pomegranate in the centre of the panel.

St Saviour (1) *(see map ref. 3)*

Title   a) Christ the Light of the World
                     b) Jesus the Bread of Life

Position   South wall, in chancel

Biblical Ref   a) John 8, verse 12
                     b) John 6, verses 30 - 58

Signature   H. T. Bosdet, Grove Park Terrace, Chiswick

Memorial Inscription

To the Glory of God and in Memory of John Gibaut, born MDCCCXXI (1821), Died MDCCCLXXXVII (1887). Given by his widow Blanche Gibaut.

Description

A double window.

In the left-hand panel, Jesus, in a striking magenta robe and crowned with thorns, holds a lantern in his right hand, under a canopy of flowering and fruiting brambles. The right-hand panel shows Jesus wearing a rich red and blue cope and holding a flat loaf of bread in his left hand. His right hand is raised in blessing and He stands under a canopy of roses.

Two smaller panels above depict brambles and roses. A third panel shows an angel holding a scroll bearing the text: "The Gentiles shall come to thy light" (Isaiah 60 verse 3).

St. Ouen's Manor Chapel,
St. Anne and Joachim at the
Golden Gate (detail)

St Saviour (2) *(see map ref.3)*

Title   a) The Man of Sorrows
                      b) The Good Shepherd

Position   South wall, in the choir

Biblical Ref   a) Matthew 27, verses 27 – 31
                      b) John 10, verses 1 – 18 and Psalm 23

Memorial Inscription

Presented by Evelina Maria Voisin, in memory of her parents John and Anne Falle of La Chasse in this Parish MDCCCCV (1905).

Description

A double window. Left-hand panel. Under a canopy of flowering and fruiting brambles and passion-flowers, Christ stands forlorn, wearing a crown of thorns and holding a reed in his bound hands. The right-hand panel shows Christ holding a shepherd's crook and carrying a lamb on his left arm. He is surrounded by sheep, under a canopy of roses.

There are three smaller panels above, two of which depict brambles and roses. The third shows St John the Divine as an old man with a red halo. He holds a rod from which flies a scroll bearing his words from the Book of Revelation: "I saw and bore record that this is the Son of God." (Revelation, 1 verse 34)

St Saviour (3) (see map ref.3)

Title   The Annunciation

Position   West wall, above the porch

Biblical Ref   Luke 1, verses 26 – 38

Signature

The Ecclesiastical Court granted a faculty for the installation of this window on 7th October 1907.

Memorial Inscription

To the Glory of God and in memory of John Fauvel of this parish.

Description

A double window.

On the left, the Archangel Gabriel, with flaming halo and lily in his right hand, greets the Virgin Mary.

On the right, the Virgin Mary is seated, head inclined with eyes downcast. Above her flies the dove of the Holy Ghost. A view of Nazareth can be seen through the bars of the window behind the Virgin Mary.

Both the angel and Mary are surmounted by Gothic canopies.

High above, there are four small decorative panels. A fifth panel shows an angel with the text: "Behold, from henceforth all generations shall call me blessed." (Luke 1, verse 48)

St.Martin's Church,
The Sacrifice of Isaac (detail)

St Saviour (4) <small>(see map ref.3)</small>

Title   St Martin of Tours

Position   West wall, over the northwest door

The Ecclesiastical Court granted a faculty for the installation of this window on 7th October 1907.

Memorial Inscription

There is no memorial inscription but, according to F. de l'Isle Bois, in his book "The Parish Church of St Saviour" (Phillimore, 1976), this window is probably the gift of William Dolbel and his sisters.

Description

A double window.

The window portrays a famous incident in the early life of St Martin, who, as a young soldier in Gaul, cut his cloak in two with his sword and shared it with a beggar. Martin became Bishop of Tours in 370 AD and was one of the great figures in the development of French monasticism.

On the left, Martin, in medieval costume and wearing spurs, cuts his cloak with his sword. Behind him rise the roofs, walls and towers of the city of Tours.

In the right-hand panel, two beggars face St Martin. The first, a young man, is kneeling with arms outstretched, ready to receive part of the cloak. Behind him stands a blind man, supporting himself upon a crutch.

The figures stand under canopies of Gothic architecture.

There are two small decorative panels of glass above. Two others show angels with scrolls bearing the biblical text: "Well done, thou good and faithful servant " (Matthew 25, verse 21). The whole is dominated by a fifth panel depicting a bishop's mitre and an heraldic tower, symbolising the bishopric of Tours.

St Saviour (5) *(see map ref.3)*

Title
A painted reredos representing the Nativity

Position
Behind the high altar

Biblical Ref
Luke 2, verses 1 – 20
Matthew 2, verses 1 - 12

Signature

Each of the three panels bears Bosdet's signature and the date 1907.

Description

The reredos, painted in Pre-Raphaelite style, is divided into three panels.

The central panel depicts the Holy Family, with Mary holding the Christ Child standing on her knees. The panel on the left shows the adoration of the Magi and the right-hand panel represents the arrival of the shepherds. The figures and buildings are all painted against a gilded background.

St.Saviour's Church, detail of the reredos

Further Reading

The following publications have proved invaluable to me while I was researching the life and work of Henry Thomas Bosdet. Without exception, they are readily accessible to the non-specialist and make fascinating reading.

A   Local Background Reading:

- Balleine, Biographical Dictionary of Jersey, Staples 1948
- Payne's Armorial of Jersey 1865
- John McCormack, Channel Island Churches, Phillimore & Co., 1986
- Warwick Rodwell, The Fishermen's Chapel, Société Jersiaise, 1990
- Raoul Lemprière, Buildings and Memorials of the Channel Islands, Hale, London, 1980
- Francis Parkinson Keyes, St Anne, Allan Wingate, 1956

B   Stained glass:

- J.D.Le Couteur, English Medieval Painted Glass, SPCK 1926
- Dr John Taylor, Stained Glass in Jersey's Churches, a comprehensive series of articles which appeared monthly in Jersey's Church of England magazine "The Pilot" between 1993 and 1995.
- Michael Archer, English Stained Glass, HMSO, Victoria and Albert Museum, 1985
- June Osborne, Stained Glass in England, Frederick Muller Ltd., 1985

Bosdet's Tomb, Northern Perimeter of the Old Cemetery, St.Saviour's Church

Epilogue

This guide book is limited to Bosdet's windows in Jersey and gives details of his life as we know them to date. Much remains, however, to be discovered, both of the man himself and of his windows outside the Island.

Below is a list of his known windows outside Jersey. Visitors to the Island who have knowledge of the whereabouts of any Bosdet windows in the UK, or elsewhere, are invited to contact the Curator of Art, Jersey Heritage Trust, Jersey Museum, St Helier, JERSEY JE2 3NF.

All information, which will be gratefully acknowledged, will be of help in building up a complete list of Bosdet's works.

- Bishopbourne, Kent   St Mary's Church
- Barbados,   Legislative Buildings
- Câtel, Guernsey   Ste Marie du Câtel
- Child Okeford, Dorset   St Nicholas Church
- Easebourne, West Sussex   St Mary's Church
- Greenhead, Northumberland   St Cuthbert's Church
- Highcliffe, Hants
- Hexham, Northumberland   Hexham Abbey
- Kensington, London   St George's Church
- Kingsclere, Hampshire   St Mary's Church
- Pinchbeck, Lincs   St Mary's Church
- South Mimms, Herts   St Giles' Church
- Swineshead, Lincs   St Mary's Church
- Terwick, Sussex   St Peter's Church
- Upton St Leonard's, Glos
- Utrecht, The Netherlands   Holy Trinity Church

In addition to the location of his windows, we need to know more of the man himself, his childhood and relationship with his parents, his school days and years as a student, his private life as a family man, his philosophy of art and his years with the Royal Academy, the influence upon his work of the Pre-Raphaelites and other contemporary artists and movements, the organisation of his workshops and so on. What was his standing among the numerous stained glass artists of his time? What evaluation can we make of his work in the broad context of late nineteenth and early twentieth century stained glass design and production?

For some strange reason, this distinguished Jerseyman has sunk into near oblivion. There is no plaque honouring his memory and his tomb in St Saviour's Cemetery, with its inscription rendered illegible by time, badly needs repair.

The year 2006 will be the 150th anniversary of his birth. It would be a fitting occasion to celebrate his talent and to ensure that Bosdet finally acquires his rightful place among Jersey's outstanding sons and daughters.

Credits

Text and photographs of windows - Aidan Smith
Photography of cartoons - Robin Briault for the Jersey Heritage Trust
Photographs of HTB, aged 50 and of his father Captain Bosdet,
Courtesy of Société Jersiaise Photographic Archive.
Photographs of the Bosdet family - Courtesy of Paul Bosdet,
Carnforth, Lancashire.

St.Mary's Church,
Nativity Window (detail)

Acknowledgments

In researching and producing this account of the life and work of Henry Thomas Bosdet, I have received generous and enthusiastic help from a great number of sources which I now acknowledge with gratitude.

This publication would not have been possible without the support of Jersey Tourism, the Jersey Arts Trust and the Jersey Heritage Trust and a small number of individual sponsors. The generous encouragement and advice of Elizabeth Jeffreys, Donna Le Marrec, Chris Clifford and Jonathan Carter have been invaluable. Their appreciation of the significance for Jersey of Henry Thomas Bosdet's work has been crucial for the success of this project. I am greatly indebted, too, to Louise Downie, Curator of Art at the Jersey Heritage Trust, for her faith in the project, her encouragement and her suggestions concerning the text of the book.

My warm thanks go to all those responsible for the beautiful churches which were my place of work for eighteen months or so: The Dean of Jersey, the Rectors, Vicars, Priests-in-Charge, Churchwardens, Administrators, Vergers, Church Archivists and Caretakers, all who have made me and my camera so welcome.

Along with them I thank Philip Malet de Carteret, Seigneur of St Ouen and Mrs Malet de Carteret for so kindly allowing me to photograph the Bosdet windows in the Manor and in the chapel and for permitting the use of some of those photographs in this publication.

I am indebted to the following persons for their valued help and encouragement which came in so many forms:

Deidre Shute, *President of The Société Jersiaise*
Pauline Syvret, *Executive Director, The Société Jersiaise*
Clive Barton, *Treasurer, The Société Jersiaise*
Jonathan Voak *of the Société Jersiaise Publications Committee*
Dr Ralph Nichols, *Société Jersiaise Publications Committee*
K. W. Syvret MBE, *Greffier of the Ecclesiastical Court*
Doug Ford, *Head of Community Learning, Jersey Heritage Trust*
Colin Dallison, *Archivist at Hexham Abbey, Northumberland*
Sue Clayton, *Churchwarden, St Nicholas Church, Child Okeford, Dorset*
Nigel & Alison Wildsmith, *Pickering, Yorkshire*

Arnold Rietveld, Archivist, Holy Trinity Church, Utrecht
Robert Eberhard, Researcher, 19th and 20th century stained glass, Epsom, UK
Peter Batts, UK
Alec C Podger
Dr John Taylor, author of many articles on Jersey's stained glass heritage.
Paul Bosdet, genealogist of the Bosdet family, Carnforth, Lancashire
Brian Vibert
Helier Smith
John Blench FRGS
K. J. Durham MA, Headmaster, University College School, Hampstead
Roger Jones, Hon. Editor, Jersey Society in London Bulletin
Anne Harrison, Assistant Librarian, Victoria College, Jersey
Elspeth Legg, Librarian, Beaulieu Convent School
Roger Jones, Editor, The Jersey Society in London Bulletin
Brian Ahier Read, The Jersey Society in London

I have been greatly assisted by various local and national archives, whose members of staff have been unfailingly courteous, patient and interested in the project. First and foremost, I must mention Angela Underwood and Anna Baghiani, the Librarian and Assistant Librarian of The Lord Coutanche Library of the Société Jersiaise, whose enthusiasm and persistence knew no bounds. Their contribution and that of the following bodies deserve my heartfelt thanks.

The Royal Academy
The Victoria and Albert Museum
The National Portrait Gallery
The Worshipful Company of Master Glaziers and Painters of Glass
The British Society of Master Glass Painters
The Guildhall Museum
The Royal Maritime Museum, Greenwich
The Public Records Office, Kew
University of Liverpool Archives
Memorial University of Newfoundland
The Borough Libraries of Chiswick, Hendon, Isleworth and Marylebone
Cork County Library
The Archive of the Jersey Heritage Trust
The Jersey Library
The Parish Administrations of St Helier, St Lawrence and St Peter, Jersey
The Office of the Registrar General, Jersey
The Land Registry Office, Jersey